Anonymous

Dr. O'Dwyer, Roman Catholic Bishop of Limerick, and the Irish nationalists

A statement of facts in connection with Mr. John Dillon's attack on the

Rev. Dr. O'Dwyer

Anonymous

Dr. O'Dwyer, Roman Catholic Bishop of Limerick, and the Irish nationalists
A statement of facts in connection with Mr. John Dillon's attack on the Rev. Dr. O'Dwyer

ISBN/EAN: 9783337124892

Printed in Europe, USA, Canada, Australia, Japan

Cover: Foto ©ninafisch / pixelio.de

More available books at **www.hansebooks.com**

DR. O'DWYER,

ROMAN CATHOLIC BISHOP OF LIMERICK,

AND THE

IRISH NATIONALISTS.

[A Statement of facts in connection with Mr. John Dillon's attack on the Rev. Dr. O'Dwyer.]

LONDON:
P. S. KING AND SON,
PARLIAMENTARY BOOKSELLERS,
5, KING STREET, WESTMINSTER.

NOVEMBER, 1890.
E 1

[481

POPE AND PRELATE.

RESCRIPT OR REVOLUTION.

THE following is a summary of events connected
with a serious scandal which occurred in Ireland
in the latter end of August, 1890, when an Irish
Catholic Bishop was publicly insulted in his own
Cathedral City, by men who are leading members
of the Parnellite party, and who profess to call
themselves Roman Catholics. A very few words
will be necessary to show how the scandal arose.

It will be recollected that during April, 1888,
His Holiness the Pope saw fit to issue a Decree
of Holy Office which he himself ratified, and by
which Boycotting and the Plan of Campaign were
formally and authoritatively condemned.

The following is a translation of the Brief or
Rescript which contains the Decree in question.

THE PAPAL DECREE.

" On several occasions the Apostolic See has given
to the people of Ireland (whom it has always regarded
with special benevolence) suitable admonitions and
advice, when circumstances required, as to how they
might defend their rights without injury to justice or
to the public peace.

[483

" Our Holy Father. Leo XIII., fearing lest in that species of warfare that has been introduced amongst the Irish people into the contests between landlords and tenants, and which is commonly called the Plan of Campaign, and in that kind of social interdict called boycotting, arising from the same contests, true sense of justice and charity might be perverted, ordered the Supreme Congregation of the Inquisition to subject the matter to serious and careful examination.

" Hence the following question was proposed to their Eminences the Cardinals of that Congregation :— Is it permissible, in the disputes between landowners and tenants in Ireland to use the means known as the Plan of Campaign and boycotting ? After long and mature deliberation their Eminences unanimously answered in the negative, and the decision was confirmed by the Holy Father on Wednesday, the 18th of the present month.

" The justice of this decision will be readily seen by anyone who applies his mind to consider that a rent agreed on by mutual consent cannot, without violation of a contract, be diminished at the mere will of tenant, especially when there are tribunals appointed for settling such controversies and reducing unjust rents within the bounds of equity, after taking into account the causes which diminish the value of the land.

" Neither can it be considered permissible that rents be extorted from tenants and deposited in the hands of unknown persons to the detriment of the land-owners. Finally, it is contrary to justice and charity to persecute by a social interdict those who are satisfied to pay the rents they agreed to, or those who, in the exercise of their right, take vacant farms.

" It will, therefore, be your Lordship's duty, pru-dently, but effectively, to advise and exhort the clergy and the laity not to transgress the bounds of Christian

charity and justice whilst they are striving for a remedy
for their distressed condition.

(Signed) "R. Cardinal Monaco.
"Rome, *April 20th*, 1888."

It is needless to follow in detail the events which
took place after this irrevocable, but most natural, act
on the part of the Supreme Pontiff. The Parnellites
resisted His Holiness, and publicly and strenuously
enforced, as far as they were able, their immoral and
illegal proceedings with relentless vigour.

One Irish Bishop took a simple course in this
emergency, Dr. O'Dwyer, Bishop of Limerick, openly
taught the Papal Rescript, and sought to carry it into
effect. He strove bravely and nobly in the face of
difficulties, which none can appreciate but himself, and
he boldly told his people that sin is to be avoided in
whatever shape it may present itself to the passions of
unfortunate and deluded humanity.

Now, in the Limerick Diocese there had been
established the Plan of Campaign upon an estate
called Glensharrold, before the issue of the Papal
Decree. The Bishop took every means to put an end
to it, and with this object he wrote a final letter to the
Parish Priest of the tenants on the estate. This letter
proved to be the commencement of a phase of outrage
against Episcopal authority, which is described in the
following pages. The letter, which is here reproduced,
was addressed to the Ven. Archdeacon Halpin, V.G.,
and incidentally gives the whole case in dispute
between landlord and tenant.

It will be only necessary to say that the Glensharrold Estate is situated within four miles of the
railway station of Ardagh, and about thirty Irish
miles from Limerick. The Estate is owned by
Mr. John C. Delmege, who purchased it in 1853.
Mr. Delmege mortgaged the property to the Scottish

Union and National Assurance Company, and, falling
into arrears with the Interest, the Estate was placed
by the mortgagees under the Court of Chancery.
There are about thirty tenants and twenty lotholders
or squatters on the Estate.

THE PALACE, CORBALLY,

LIMERICK, 19*th May*, 1890.

MY DEAR ARCHDEACON,—I have learned that the judges
of the Landed Estates Court have determined to make no
further advance on the concessions which they offered through
me last January to the Glensharrold tenantry, and unless
these terms are accepted at once that they will proceed to
eviction. Now this is a great calamity. All through these
negotiations I hoped that our poor people would be spared
the miseries of it, and now that it is at their doors I make this
last appeal to them as their friend and their bishop. I beg of
them in their own interest to accept the court's offer and keep
the roof over their heads. Last January I told them that I
thought it not only a fair but a liberal offer, and that in my
opinion they would be guilty of reckless folly in rejecting it.
I repeat that opinion, and I am confident that when the
public come to know the facts of the case, and the obstinacy
of those who decline to accept, they will condemn it, and still
more severely the mischievous cruelty of those parties who
are egging them on to destruction. It would be well to point out
again to these poor people that the rent which they are now asked
to pay has not been fixed by the landlord or by anyone who
has a sixpence interest in it. It has been determined by the
Judges of the Landed Estates Court, on the report of their
own valuer, the Chief Receiver in Chancery, who came in
person on the estate for the purpose. I know that he was
instructed to do justice to the tenants. I know that he went
upon the land animated with the largest sympathy with them,
and a determination to treat them liberally. Now, whatever
he said about the tenants combining against rapacious and
oppressive landlords there can be no justification of their
resisting the decision of the highest tribunal in the land, that
has been reached through the advice of as competent a land
valuer and as honourable a man as there is in all Ireland.
Then ask the tenants to consider what is offered to them.
They should remember that they are judicial leaseholders,
486]

and that the court for the first time, as far as I know, in Ireland proposes to put aside these judicial leases and refix the fair rent. That is a very strong thing to do, and they do it thoroughly. Off the rents reserved in the judicial leases they make an abatement of 30 per cent. all round, and that without compensation of any kind to the landlord. Mr. Parnell, the other day in the House of Commons, proposed that the Government should lend money to the landlords as an inducement to them to reduce the judicial rents of all tenants who are valued at under £50 a year exactly by this sum. Is it not a noteworthy comment on his proposition that on the first property on which it is tried, tenants of the very class he contemplates are instructed to refuse that settlement, even though landlords get no compensation? But, apart from general considerations such as these, can the tenants expect public sympathy and public approval in rejecting such an offer as the following:—(1) They owe five years' arrears, for which they will get a clear receipt on the payment of one year's rent, less 30 per cent. (2) They are allowed to surrender judicial leases, which reduced their rents on an average by 25 per cent., and they will get a further reduction of 30 per cent., that is bringing their future rent about 50 per cent. under their old rent. The figures stand thus :—

Arrears due to March, 1890, £2,611 14s. 9d.
Payment to be accepted, £384 11s.
Arrears to be forgiven, £2,227 3s. 9d.

Rents—Old rent, £738 15s. 4d. ; judicial, £542 6s. ; present offer of judges, £384 11s. ; gross annual reduction, £354 4s. 4d.

Now, it will be impossible on these figures to persuade the public that these poor people are still the victims of rapacious landlordism, or that they have any just cause for taking the extreme and, for them, terrible step of abandoning their homes. If they have sense they will do nothing of the kind. Even supposing that their own demand of 40 per cent. instead of 30 per cent. were reasonable they would not be justified, for so small a sum, in bringing upon themselves the sorrow and heartbreak of eviction and disturbing the whole side of a country. ● It only means a difference of £54 a year between forty-seven tenants, and surely sensible men are not going to break up their little homes and scatter their stock for a sum like that. To the largest farmer on the estate it means only £7 10s. a year. His old rent was £100, his judicial rent is £75. The court's offer now to him is £52 10s. He is willing to pay

[487

£45. I ask any sensible man if it is a reasonable proceeding of that tenant to sacrifice everything, even though he might reasonably expect to get the further reduction ? Would it not be better for him to put his £57 10s. a year in his pocket and hold his land. For many of the tenants the difference does not amount to £1 a year, and surely, right or wrong, they are not justified in throwing up their poor homes for that. I beg of them then, at the last moment, before taking a step which they may regret all the days of their lives, to listen to my advice. If they spend a year in idleness on the side of the road, neither they nor their children will ever raise their heads again. The farmer whose home is once broken up, whose stock is scattered and his capital spent, may recover his lands after some years, but he will be a pauper while he lives. In this case, if the tenants go out, I can see no prospect of their return for many a day. They are dealing, not with a landlord, but with the judges of the Landed Estates Court, and it is not easy to see how the court can be brought in a case like this to reverse its own action. You know, my dear Archdeacon, and all the priests of this diocese know, that my policy has been uniformly to help the people to get as large reductions of rent as possible, for I have always held that rents were too high, but at the same time I have advised everyone concerned, when "all went to all," to keep the roof over their people's heads. I say the same now to the people of Glensharrold. They have got immense concessions. They have a fair way of living. Let them not now by one supreme act of folly throw away all that they have gained. Thus urging them to cling to their homes, I have but one end in view, and that is their own good. It would be easy for me to win popularity by taking another course, but even if higher motives did not restrain me I should be ashamed to ask poor people to endure the heartbreaking sorrows of eviction which I had no notion of ever undergoing myself.—I am, my dear Archdeacon, very faithfully yours in Christ,

✠ EDWARD THOMAS,
Bishop of Limerick.

This letter produced a good deal of angry feeling on the part of those who were determined to advocate

the condemned practices as their sole programme for
the "regeneration of Ireland." But another incident
occurred about this time which aroused the animosity
of the Separatist party. Last winter a British Mission
was sent with due ceremony to the Holy See to
negotiate certain matters which concerned Malta.
Strange as it may appear at first sight, this event
aroused the fierce resentment of the Parnellite party,
and a great deal of anger was displayed both against
the Pope and against the British Government.
Mr. T. M. Healy, M.P., taunted the House of
Commons that the old "No Popery" cry was extinct.
But it was reserved for Mr. John Dillon, M.P., to
overstep all decency by making a speech in the House
of Commons on the 11th July, which denounced both
the Pope and the Bishop of Limerick in the following
astounding language, reported by the *Freeman's
Journal*.

Mr. Dillon said :—

The Irish members had been assailed in this country as the
advocates of Home Rule in Ireland, and it had been used as an
argument against them that an Irish Parliament would inevitably
be slaves to the Pope and subservient to Rome, but what did the
Chief Secretary do? Did he not in conjunction with his uncle,
[Lord Salisbury] send to the Pope and try to bribe him to help to
crush the Irish people (loud cheers). He did not think any more
humiliating or disgusting spectacle had ever been exhibited than
the right hon. gentleman standing before a Manchester audience
and rebuking the Catholics of Ireland for not showing sufficient
deference to the head of their Church (loud laughter). Speaking
then as an Irish Catholic and on behalf of the Catholics of Ireland,
he told the right hon. gentleman that he and his co-religionists were
as independent of Rome and of the agents of his Holiness in all
political matters as any Nonconformist sitting on those benches
(cheers). They were far more independent in political matters
of Rome than the right hon. gentleman and his uncle were, who
debased the honour of England by crawling to the Court of
Rome and offering bribes to His Holiness to aid them in crushing
the people of Ireland (loud cheers). There was no fouler stain
cast on the people of England, and no more intolerable grievance
inflicted on the people of Ireland, than when the right hon.

gentleman succeeded in getting His Holiness to send an agent to
trade on the reverence of the Irish people. They would never
allow his promises for one single hour to interfere between them
and the goal on which they had set their hopes (loud cheers),
nor would they allow him to use them as a means to sow discord
between the Irish members and the Irish people. They scorned
his offers. They wanted no Catholic University from him.
What they wanted was liberty to regulate their own affairs in
Ireland. For two generations they had been denied justice in
that matter, and now they could afford to wait a little longer.
They would have the university in Ireland they desired when
they had a home Parliament. The right hon. gentleman had
succeeded by his promises and schemes in capturing two Irish
bishops, one of whom, Dr. O'Dwyer, had written a most violent
and dastardly letter.*

The CHIEF SECRETARY—I rise to order. I don't think an
attack on an Irish bishop can be properly made on this vote (oh).

The CHAIRMAN—I understood the hon. gentleman was referring
to the right hon. gentleman's action. If he went on to attack
the bishop no doubt he would not be in order (Ministerial
cheers).

Mr. DILLON—I think the action of the right hon. gentleman in
springing from his seat to defend the bishop———

The CHIEF SECRETARY—I again rise to order. I sprang from
my seat because I thought the hon. gentleman went beyond the
vote. I shall not attempt to defend the bishop (oh, oh).

Mr. DILLON said he would say no more on that point (hear,
hear). All he would say was that, as an Irish Catholic, that
gentleman had done his worst against the Irish Church, and he
was exceedingly glad he stood alone among the Episcopacy of
Ireland, with his scandalous conduct (cheers).

This speech, as was only natural, roused the honest
indignation of the Bishop of Limerick, and he
immediately wrote to the *Freeman's Journal* as
follows :—

TO THE EDITOR OF THE "FREEMAN'S JOURNAL."

SIR,—I once heard a beggar woman pouring forth the foulest
abuse in the public street on an apparently and respectable and
inoffensive looking man. My curiosity being stimulated, I inquired

---

* This portion of Mr. Dillon's speech is reported as follows in the *Daily
News* of the 12th July :—" Dr. O'Dwyer, the Catholic Bishop of Limerick, had
written a letter which was one of the most infamous, cowardly and dastardly ever
penned. The Bishop was the servant of the Government."

490]

the cause, and learned that he had informed some casual passer by, who was touched by the number and poverty of the children into giving alms, that these children in reality were not her own, but had been borrowed from a sympathetic neighbour for eleemosynary purposes—*Hinc illæ lachrymæ*. It is only in the same way that I can account for

MR. DILLON'S OUTBURST OF OUTRAGEOUS LANGUAGE

in denouncing me for the simple and matter-of-fact letter which I gave to the public on the Glensharrold case. He had been engaged labouring of late collecting money, ostensibly for the relief of evicted tenants. He and his party are still occupied in the same profitable employment, and, just as they hoped to strike another golden vein by the exhibition of death sentences ruthlessly carried out upon the hapless victims of heartless landlordism, it must have been very provoking to have the real facts of the case exposed and the pockets of the sympathisers closed. Hence I can very well understand Mr. Dillon's anger, but all the same I cannot excuse his language. He applies term of insult to me that he would not dare to use if I were a layman sitting opposite to him in the House of Commons. "Infamous, cowardly, dastardly," are the epithets by which he describes my letter, and

HE CALLS MY CONDUCT "SCANDALOUS."

Now, I never in my life said one word that was personally offensive to Mr. Dillon. For good or evil, I never even mentioned his name in public. Why, then, should he wantonly use in my regard language of so gross and insulting vituperation? In reply I tell him simply that my letter was not infamous, but the truth, and that I am no coward nor dastard, but that is the conduct of a coward and a dastard to use such language to any man, but most of all to a bishop, behind his back. I am not equal to a contest in Billingsgate with Mr. Dillon, nor do I mean to try it. But I will tell him this, that if at any time I should find myself put into prison for a cause that I professed to believe just, I would rot there before I allowed my friends to send up a miserable whine for my release from every end of the country on the plea of health, and that if I sneaked out thus and then went off to the Antipodes on a twelve months' tour until the storm blew over and my vows to defy the Act of Parliament under which I had been imprisoned were forgotten, he might call me a dastard without fear of contradiction.

But, sir, I am almost ashamed of myself to waste so many words on this gentleman's personal offensiveness to myself, when I read the language which he dares to use towards the august and sacred person of the Vicar of Christ.

IT IS NO DISGRACE, BUT AN HONOUR,

for a poor, simple bishop to receive a few spatters of the dirt that
is flung at the representative of his Divine Master. If only I could
get it all, and be covered with opprobrium while I lived, so as to
spare our old Catholic nation the shame before the world that
one of the foulest charges ever levelled against the successors of
St. Peter was hurled at Leo XIII., amidst the cheers of English
Protestants and English unbelievers by one who professes to be
a member of the Church. Why, the Giordano Bruno people do
not impeach the Pope's personal honour. M. Constans and his
colleagues in France believe in no God, and attack religion, but
they never stoop to charge the Head of the Church with
Charlatanism. But here is a Catholic boasting of his Catho-
licity, the friend of bishops and archbishops, using the
privileges of the faith in order to get near the Father of the
Faithful and stab him in the back. Let the Catholic people of
Ireland listen to this:

They were far more independent in political matters of Rome than
the right hon. gentleman and his uncle were, who debased the honour
of England by crawling to the Court of Rome and offering bribes to
his Holiness to aid them in crushing the people of Ireland. (Loud
cheers.) There was no fouler stain cast on the people of England, no
more intolerable grievance inflicted on the people of Ireland, than when
the right hon. gentleman succeeded in getting his Holiness to send an
agent to trade on the reverence of the Irish people.

Was ever so desperate, so recklessly and wildly desperate a
charge made by any Catholic in the greatest drunkenness of
excess comparable to this—that Leo XIII. trafficked in the
reverence of a Catholic people for his own purposes, pretended
to teach them the duties of the Christian life, whereas for some
bribe or other that he got from the English Government he was
leading them deliberately astray? Why, apart altogether from
his office, and that divine guidance under which he acts, if we
only think of the personality of Leo XIII. we shall see the horrible
grotesqueness of this vile accusation. In Christendom there is no
nobler figure this moment. Set in the background of sorrow that
God has allowed to gather so heavily around him, he stands a
figure of light and grandeur, the glory and the pride of the
Catholic Church. He is seated on the throne whose greatness
dwarfs all human dimensions, and yet in the force, the simplicity,
the elevation, of his personal character he has drawn the hearts
of the people in admiration to himself; and is it not pitiful to see
this poor young member of Parliament, in presence of the world,
encouraged by the cheers of men who detest the Pope because
they detest the Catholic Church, flinging insult and vituperation
492]

on him ? This gentleman has often boasted of his intimacy with bishops and archbishops, and the aid which he got from them at home and abroad. It will be interesting to observe how many of them now will be anxious to identify themselves with him publicly until this insulting slander is withdrawn.

Besides the mere scurrility of his speech there is one definite charge of Mr. Dillon's with which I should wish to deal. He states that "Mr. Balfour had secured me." That he had "captured me." What precisely does he mean by these statements? If he means that any action which I have taken in public affairs has been the result of engagement, compact, negotiation of any kind, publicly or privately, between me and the Government or Mr. Balfour, he states what is absolutely and entirely false. That is evidently what he intended to convey. That is the meaning that nineteen-twentieths of the Irish people at home and abroad will draw from his words; but you will observe at the same time that they are cautiously chosen, so as to give Mr. Dillon an escape by their innocent meaning. This is a specimen of his courage, and I invite all honourable men in Ireland to observe his future action with regard to this. They will then see the weighty evidence that this responsible gentleman had in his mind, when he levelled against an Irish bishop the charge of having been "captured" by the English Government.

No doubt

I HAVE CONDEMNED THE PLAN OF CAMPAIGN AND BOYCOTTING.

I believe them not only at variance with the very first elements of civilized life, but unjust, and boycotting in particular as essentially anti-Christian. The Supreme Head of the Church has confirmed my judgment on them. There is as little doubt for a Catholic now that the decree of the Holy Office condemning these practices, binds his conscience as that he is forbidden to eat meat on Friday. Mr. Dillon can satisfy himself of that any day by turning in and asking Cardinal Manning if it is not so. If he wants it he can get an official affirmation of it from his own bishop or archbishop in Ireland. Is it not, then, intolerable that he should denounce me in the House of Commons, and attempt to hold me up to the hatred of my countrymen as their enemy, simply for discharging my duty as a bishop, and teaching my people according to my conscience? No doubt it may have been a rash thing for me single handed to provoke the anger of Mr. Dillon and his friends. It might have been more in accordance with the secular wisdom of temporisers in all times to hold my tongue so as to escape personal annoyance. But these are all considerations for myself. The question for the public is, am I or am I not within my rights in thinking as a man, and teaching as a bishop, that the Plan of Campaign and boycotting are against the law of God? If that

[493

question is answered in the affirmative I should like to know what justification remains for

MR. DILLON'S ABOMINABLE CHARGES.

And this suggests another grave question, which I beg to submit to the consideration of thoughtful statesmen, such as Mr. Parnell, Mr. Justin M'Carthy, Mr. Sexton, and Mr. Arthur O'Connor. If Mr. Dillon, whether he has the right or not, has the power, without check or remonstrance from any one of his party, to denounce an Irish bishop as he has denounced me simply and solely for my action in the exercise of my spiritual jurisdiction, what guarantee is there, should Home Rule come, that all of us bishops shall not find our authority crippled, not by words, but by force? Are there not interests enough arrayed to the death against Home Rule to make it at least a matter of common tactical prudence not to force the bishops in Ireland to review their position in relation to it? The lawfulness or unlawfulness of the Plan of Campaign was a subject as fully within the competence of the Holy See to decide as the validity of Henry the Eighth's marriage. If we find Irish members of Parliament using against the Holy See, when they are condemned, the very language and arguments of the first English reformers—if we see a repetition, so far as their limited power goes, by Mr. Dillon and his friends of the conduct of those Englishmen who struck terror into the body of English bishops, and ran blessed Fisher into jail, may we not reasonably ask how will it be with the independence of the Irish Church—how will it be with the unfettered intercourse which we demand with Rome, when these gentlemen are not only our representatives but our masters? I commend that view of things to the consideration of serious Home Rulers, and beg of them not to drive us to compare the religious liberty we enjoy at present with the prospects of things under Mr. Dillon as Minister of Worship.

Again and again I have said I am a Home Ruler. At home and abroad I have maintained the right of my country to self-government. In so far as the agitation legitimately advances that cause I am with it. I would join it to-morrow if I had any assurance that the movement was to be purged from sinful methods, but while Mr. Dillon and men like him, in defiance of their own leader, are the practical leaders, I must only stand aloof. I may illustrate my position by a humorous incident. Some time ago great crowds attended the sermons of a revivalist here in Limerick. At the end of a very vehement discourse he called upon all those of his audience who wished to go to Heaven to stand up. All stood up except one Catholic young man, who ought not to have been there at all. "Young man," said the preacher solemnly, "do you not wish to go to Heaven?" "Oh

494]

yes, I do," said the young man, "but not with that crowd." Begging you to excuse the length to which this letter has run, I have the honour to be, sir, your obedient servant,

✠ EDWARD THOMAS,
Bishop of Limerick.

Mr. Dillon upon this replied in the following manner, in a letter also addressed to the Editor of the *Freeman's Journal.*

TO THE EDITOR OF THE "FREEMAN."

SIR,—I have no intention of making any reply to the letter of Dr. O'Dwyer, which appears in your issue of to-day. I think I am quite safe in leaving that letter to the judgment of the Irish people. The only point in it which appears to me in the least degree worthy of notice is the extract from my speech—in the concluding lines of which I am reported to have said—

"There never was a fouler stain cast upon the honour of Englana, nor a more intolerable grievance inflicted on the people of Ireland, than when the right hon. gentleman succeeded in getting his Holiness to send an agent to trade on the reverence of the Irish people."

I am quite certain I never used these words. I was speaking all along of the action of the Government of Lord Salisbury, and, so far as my memory carries me, I made no comment on any action of His Holiness. My memory in this respect is borne out by the context of my speech, by the *Times* report in which these words are not found, and by the recollection of several friends who were listening to me, and whom I have consulted on this point. —Yours sincerely,   JOHN DILLON.

July 14*th,* 1890.

The Bishop, however, having ascertained that the contradiction of Mr. Dillon was not consistent with proofs which were accessible to all, and which showed that the offensive words denied were really used in the House of Commons upon the 11th July, published these proofs in the following rejoinder to the *Freeman.*

TO THE EDITOR OF THE "FREEMAN."

Limerick, 26th July, 1890.

SIR,—May I trouble you to print, and if possible side by side the two following extracts. One is taken from Mr. Dillon's letter

[495

which you published on 15th inst., the other from Hansard's Parliamentary report of Mr. Dillon's speech on 11th inst.:—

MR. DILLON'S LETTER.

I think I am quite safe in leaving that letter to the judgment of the Irish people. The only point in it which appears to me in the least degree worthy of notice is the extract from my speech, in the concluding lines of which I am reported to have said: "There never was a fouler stain cast upon the honour of England, nor a more intolerable grievance inflicted on the people of Ireland, than when the right honourable gentleman succeeded in getting His Holiness to send an agent to trade on the reverence of the Irish people." I am quite certain I never used those words.

HANSARD'S REPORT, JULY 11, 1890 (1498).

I can tell him that we are far more independent in political matters of the Court of Rome than he and his uncle, who have debased the character of Englishmen by crawling to the Pope and offering bribes to His Holiness to aid in crushing the Catholic people of Ireland, and to inflict an intolerable wrong.

To some extent it succeeded, *when an agent was brought from Rome to go among the people and to trade on their reverence for the Church to crush their political aspirations.*

The italics are mine. Now, sir, I think few will have the hardihood to deny that this evidence puts beyond all cavil the accuracy of your representative's report of Mr. Dillon's speech, and imposes on Mr. Dillon the necessity of offering some explanation of it consistent with his veracity. It is a very serious position for any public man to occupy, and one from which no vicarious flinging of dirt will ever extricate him.

I have the honour to be, sir,

Your obedient servant,

EDWARD THOMAS,
Bishop of Limerick.

It may be well to remark here that "Hansard" Parliamentary Reports are not published until some days after the date of the proceedings they record, and that Members have an opportunity of revising their speeches.

Mr. Dillon took no notice of the Bishop's letter just given. Meanwhile an attempt was made in Limerick itself to bring popular clamour to support

Mr. Dillon, and to denounce the Bishop. These efforts were only partially successful, notwithstanding the well-known fact that Irish local bodies are nearly all composed of the nominees of the National League. In the Limerick Corporation, extremely Nationalist in its opinion, a motion condemning Dr. O'Dwyer was defeated by a majority, much to the chagrin of the Parnellites; more vigourous measures were then determined upon; the Limerick branch of the League revenged themselves upon the "unpatriotic" majority of the Corporation by finally expelling them from their ranks, and the leaders of the League arranged to attack Dr. O'Dwyer in his own Cathedral city. A great demonstration accordingly took place in Limerick on Sunday, 24th August, calculated most seriously to impair that pastoral liberty which a Bishop is always supposed to enjoy in a Christian land, and to interfere with his decisions upon moral questions. A large concourse of people attended, whipped up from the South of Ireland, and conveyed together by special trains. It appears, however, that the most respectable persons of Limerick and elsewhere (Nationalist in politics) refused to participate in this most shameful meeting. There were some thirteen Parnellite Members of Parliament present, all so called Catholics. The Member for the City (Mr. Francis A. O'Keeffe) presided. Mr. Dillon and Mr. Wm. O'Brien, the principal authors of the Plan of Campaign, were the chief speakers. All Priests were naturally absent from the scene. The speeches deserve perusal, they will afford an insight into the real forces at work in Ireland for the advancement of Parnellism.

MR. DILLON.

Mr. JOHN DILLON said so far as I myself am concerned I never had occasion to defend my character before the people of Ireland, and I never wish (cheers). It would take a greater man than

the Bishop of Limerick (groans) to put me on my defence (cheers).
I tell you from my heart, and I tell you the simple truth when I
say that if it were merely a question of my private character you
would not see me here to-day. I would not come to Limerick
to-day to defend my character or the character of any one of my
colleagues. I come here to give to the people of Limerick and
Munster the opportunity of judging between our policy and the
policy of the Bishop (cheers and groans). I come here to ask
the people of Munster whether in politics—I speak not of religion
—but whether in politics they are prepared to follow our leadership (cheers and cries of "We are"), or the leadership of the
Bishop of Limerick (no, and cheers). If the result of this meeting
left the slightest doubt upon my mind as to the feelings of the
people of Munster on this issue—that is, the political issue—you
would hear of me no more in Irish politics. I say, then, that the
great significance of this meeting is this, that you are here in
your tens of thousands (cheers) to tell the Irish nation and the
scattered Irish race in millions all over the world who will read
of this meeting to-morrow, that your confidence in the Irish party
is unshaken (loud cheers) and that you don't believe that

WE ARE SWINDLERS AND ROBBERS

of the people (cheers). You have been told that we are collecting
money to put in our own pockets (no) and make profit out of this
agitation (groans and no). Well, the people of Ireland will
know what is the deliberate judgment of the Catholic people of
Munster (loud cheers). I see around me to-day tens of
thousands of people who are as devoted to the Catholic Church
as any in the world, or as their fathers who had shed their blood
and parted with every bit of property rather than forsake their
religion (cheers). I see men around me who know what devotion
means and who are ready to-morrow if the occasion demanded
to make the same sacrifice (loud cheers) which their fathers did
for their religion (cheers). But while they are as devoted to the
Catholic Church as any in the world ("and more so") they are
as free in politics as any in the world (cheers), and they have
proved on more than one occasion how well they know to draw the
line between politics and religion (cheers). Well, I say you know
how to draw the line between politics and religion ; let me say this
also, that I scorn the man who talks of opposition between Irishmen's religion and Irishmen's politics (loud cheers). There is no
opposition between them, and the man who is a good Catholic is
a good Nationalist (cheers), and the best Nationalists are, to my
own knowledge, very frequently the best Catholics, too (cheers).
Many of those men who are finding fault with us to-day would, I

think, if a bitter persecution came, be found deserting the Church (hear, hear). They are what we might call

FAIR WEATHER RELIGION PEOPLE.

Let me say just one word to state to you accurately what it is that gave rise to that unhappy controversy between myself and the members of the Irish Party on the one side and the Bishop of Limerick on the other (groans). **I used some very strong language which it might have been better for me not to have used to a man holding so high and sacred a position, but what I say is this, that I am not here to withdraw or explain anything whatever** (loud cheers). I say this, that the people of Ireland, the Irish Catholics should know exactly what occurred (hear, hear). I used that language in reference to one single act of the Bishop's, and that was just when he wrote a letter to the *Freeman's Journal* to justify the eviction of the Glensharrold tenants (groans), and to state that these poor people deserved no public sympathy in their misfortune(groans). When I read that letter in the *Freeman*, side by side with the account of the eviction, **I must confess it made my blood boil** (cheers) **to think that a Catholic could be found in Ireland, no matter what were the merits of the case, to justify the eviction of his own people. Well, I used very strong epithets in characterising that act, and I still believe that I was justified in using that language** (cheers). But it is perfectly open to debate whether I was justified or not in that opinion. Since I used that language the Bishop (groans) has published an extraordinary document in which he charges not only myself but all the members of the Irish Party who have worked along with me in the Plan of Campaign with a variety of detestable crimes, and has made villainous charges much of the same character as those which have been levelled against our party by the most ignorant and rabid of the Tory party in England and by the late lamented *Times* newspaper (laughter and cheers).

Well, for my part, I have not the slightest intention of entering into a controversy with his lordship. The issue between us is an exceedingly simple one. I, on my part, have done nothing but condemn an act which to me appears to be a baneful and outrageous one for a Catholic Bishop to do (loud cheers). High and sacred as his office is, I say that so long as I possess the confidence of the Irish people I am justified in expressing my opinion on any act committed by his lordship when he becomes a politician and takes an active part in politics (cheers). On the other hand, his lordship has stated deliberately to the people of Ireland, in a

[499

written letter, that in his opinion I and, recollect, other members of our party with whom he had no quarrel whatever, were swindlers of the lowest type, and men who did not hesitate to plunder the poor for their own benefit (loud groans), men who were false to their pledges, false to their country, and deserving of the execration of all mankind (renewed groaning). That is the deliberate opinion of

THE BISHOP OF LIMERICK ;

and, as I said already, it is for the Irish people to judge between us (prolonged cheering). The only thing I shall say further in reference to the painful incident is this, that while it is to all of us, to you, I am sure, as it is to me, a most painful and humiliating thing to find even one Irish Catholic Bishop capable of such acts and uttering such words at the present day, we have at least this consolation, that there never was a time in the history of the Irish National struggle when the Irish Episcopacy was so national and so sound (loud cheers), and that the appeal that Dr. O'Dwyer addressed to the other bishops of Ireland to stand by his side against that execrable ruffian John Dillon (prolonged cheering), that appeal has not been answered, and it will not be answered (renewed cheers), for there is not one bishop in Ireland who will take his stand by the side of Dr. O'Dwyer and adopt his sentiments (enthusiastic cheers). The day is gone by, and I thank God for it, when anyone can sow dissension between the religion of the Irish people and the nationality of the Irish people, which it has always been our proudest boast have been kept in harmony, bound together by links which no Government and no coercion can tear asunder (cheers). The religion and nationality of the Irish people are bound to-day by stronger bonds than ever, which no power. whether it be a Catholic bishop or a Coercion Government, will ever sunder (cheers).

Mr. Dillon ended his speech by a panegyric on boycotting.

MR. WM. O'BRIEN.

Mr. WILLIAM O'BRIEN, M.P., who was enthusiastically welcomed, said—Fellow countrymen, you have proved once again to-day that the people of Limerick have never been called upon to strike a blow for Ireland without proving themselves worthy of men and of women who once held the walls of Limerick against assailants a little more formidable than the Most Rev. Dr. O'Dwyer. It seems laughable enough to mention in the same breath to an Irish crowd the name of John Dillon and the name of Bishop O'Dwyer (laughter). It is a cruel thing you should be called upon so soon again to defend yourself against the restless spirit of antagonism to the Irish cause which is for ever lurking in the midst of you in a quarter from which you are entitled to expect sympathy, and to
500]

which you would only too gladly extend reverence and love. But
the question has been forced upon you, and to-day, in the heart of
his own diocese, and from the flower of the Catholic community
of Limerick, Dr. O'Dwyer has received an answer and a rebuke,
the most moderate, but the most solemn and most irresistible that
ever sounded in the ear of an Irish prelate. We do not for one
moment grudge Dr. O'Dwyer (cheers) his right to think or say
anything he chooses. Not for a moment. What we object to is
his habit of turning a question of politics into a question of
religion the moment the argument goes against himself (hear,
hear, and applause).

DR. O'DWYER, THE POLITICIAN,

has a perfect right to hold his own opinion about us, and the Irish
people have just as good a right to hold their own opinion about
Dr. O'Dwyer (hear, hear). But he is not content with that, for
whenever he finds that the Irish people are not going to take their
politics from him, are not going to dip in the same dish with the
Balfours (groans) and with the Delmeges (groans) he turns round
and he clothes himself in the sacred garb of the episcopacy, and
he anathematises as enemies to religion every man who differs
from him, and he takes every attack that is made upon his own
mischievous political pranks as if it were an attack upon the person
of the Supreme Pontiff himself (cheers). That is what we come here
to-day to protest against, and we come not so much as Nationalists
as Catholics, for if we were enemies of religion we would only be
too proud to stand up and to chuckle when men like Dr. O'Dwyer
are introducing into Ireland these fatal elements of discord which
have the power of religion over some of the fairest province of
the country; but the faith of our fathers is as dear to the men
who are listening to me to-day as it is to Dr. O'Dwyer (cheers,
and cries of "more so"), and if that faith has been saved from
the attacks of irreligion in Ireland to-day, it is because in every
hour of danger independent Catholic laymen like Mr. Dillon
(cheers)—aye, and like heroic prelates that I could name (cries
of "Archbishop Croke and Archbishop Walsh")—have risen up,
have confronted and confounded every endeavour to turn the faith
for which Ireland suffered centuries of long martyrdom and dis-
honour, into the handmaid of the coercionist and exterminator of
the Irish people (cheers). As far as John Dillon is concerned, the
libels, the abominable and filthy libels, that have been poured out
upon him can only soil, can only sully the lips that uttered them
(cheers). I venture to say that, as a politician, if you were to seek
out a specimen of a cranky and cross-grained Irish politician it is
Dr. O'Dwyer. He is always safe to be on the opposite side to us,
and his friendship is likely to be an absolute harbinger of failure
to every cause which has the misfortune to incur his friendship

[501

(cheers). His whole life, meantime, has been a graveyard strewn with the dead bones of his failures and blunders (cheers).

THE CAMPAIGNERS ON THE GLENSHARROLD ESTATE

had a cause so absolutely just that the Bishop himself was obliged through his Vicar-General to exempt them from the operation of Monsignor Persico's mission*—that is to say, in the only case in his diocese where the Plan of Campaign was in force he was obliged to admit that Monsignor Persico was absolutely wrong, and that the Plan of Campaign was absolutely right (cheers)—that Plan of Campaign which I have never hesitated to defend in the open day, and which I am prouder to-day than ever to defend from this platform (loud cheers). Very well, the Bishop saw he was in a dilemma, and he tried to get out of it by patching up an agreement of his own and forcing the tenants to adopt it. Now, he went down unauthorised and uninvited, and he tried to intimidate the tenantry into accepting his agreement by telling them that their leaders would desert them and leave them to starve. He tried even to purchase their assent by offering to subscibe the sum of £100 to the sum they were to pay for their miserable rack rents, and he did all that man could do openly and secretly to drag these tenants into an agreement which was

CONDEMNED BY HIS OWN VALUER, MR. GREENE-BARRY

(cheers), and then what followed? He failed, as he invariably does (cheers). The people stuck to their leaders. They stuck to their rights, and then what happened? Because these people, whose cause was so just that they were exempted from the strictures of the Rescript, these people who were so poor that he felt obliged to subscribe £100 to eke out their rack rents, because these miserable, these wronged people refused to be led by him into an agreement condemned by his own valuer, he came out in the *Times* newspaper on the morning of the eviction campaign with a letter which was directly calculated to rob the Glensharrold tenantry of that English sympathy which he knew was their only safety and only protection against the blows of the exterminator (cheers). That was the transaction which John Dillon condemns (cheers), and I venture to say deliberately here to-day that a more unworthy, a more cruel, and a more shameful transaction no Irish prelate ever had to answer for before, and God forbid that any Irish prelate should ever have to answer again (loud cheers). Dr. O'Dwyer tells us that he is

"NOT GOING TO HEAVEN WITH OUR CROWD"

(laughter). Well, that is a sort of pleasantry with a smack of

---

* Monsignor Persico was the Apostolic Commissioner sent by the Pope to Ireland in the summer of 1887.

irreverence that I confess I would have thought more worthy of
a revivalist like Fiddler Joss than of a Catholic bishop (cheers).
But let me just remind his lordship that our crowd contains not
only five-sixths of the Irish people and of their representatives,
aye, nineteen-twentieths of the flower and substance of the Irish
race throughout the world, but our crowd contains also nine-
tenths of the beloved bishops and archbishops of Ireland (cheers)
—men whose sanctity will bear comparison even with Dr.
O'Dwyer's, and of whose wisdom the Irish people have had
somewhat better proofs (loud cheers). That is our crowd
(cheers). As far as we are concerned, our crowd will sweep
onward without him, and will conquer in spite of him (loud
cheers), and the day will come when possibly Dr. O'Dwyer
himself may recognise that the Catholic laymen of Limerick
have to-day taken the true means, the manly means, of preserving
that life-giving and affectionate union of faith and nationality
which runs through the blood of the Irish race (loud cheers),
and for which Sarsfield once held the walls of Limerick against
renegades within the walls as well as against King William
and Dutchmen outside (prolonged cheers).—*Freeman's Journal*,
25th August, 1890.

The proceedings of the 24th August terminated by
a dinner given that same evening in one of the hotels
in Limerick, at which the heroes of the demonstration
were present ; public speeches took place, some
sentences from which are well worth recording.

MR. WM. O'BRIEN'S REMARKS.

Mr. Wm. O'Brien : He should only say one word in reference
to the demonstration of that day, which to his mind was a
splendid specimen of the spirit of sturdiness of independence
(cheers), which was rapidly converting what was only an after-
dinner sentiment of " Ireland a nation " into a patent, a tangible,
and an irresistible reality (applause). The people of Limerick
had, he thought, shown to-day, and that without disrespect to the
sacred garb of an ecclesiastic (cheers) that no amount of canvass-
ing, no amount of ear-wigging, or of threats (cheers) could
prevent the people of Limerick from taking the measure of a
politician who was the hero of the *Limerick Chronicle* and the darling
of the County Club (cheers). They were intolerant, forsooth, because some of them had been naughty enough to expel from the
National League, and to promise to expel from the Corporation
as well, the men who acquiesced in the imputations upon John
Dillon (cheers) So the people of Dublin were intolerant when

they drove out of the corporation of Dublin the men who refused the freedom of Dublin to Charles Stewart Parnell (applause). But they did it and the result was, that the Dublin Corporation was to-day one of the impregnable strongholds of Irish nationality (cheers). God knew no man longed and pined more earnestly than he did for the time when this strife of theirs would be over and when there would be the fullest liberty for the widest differences. They were in the midst of a struggle for the very life of their nation—a struggle in which the great Archbishop of Cashel (loud cheers) once told them there must be no neutrals (cheers) . . . They took the consequences, and so must those who dared not utter one word of honest protest when John Dillon was publicly assailed as a swindler and poltroon (cheers). **These men defended themselves upon the whimpering plea that they were Catholics first and Irishmen afterwards** ("oh!"). **He said that cry was a fraudulent and dishonest cry** (loud cheers). They might as well talk of being men of flesh first and men of blood afterwards, or being men with a right leg first and a left leg afterwards. The men who would defend themselves for being bad Irishmen on the score of being good Catholics were simply men who were cowardly trimmers first (loud cheers) and slaves and hypocrites and renegades after (cheers). As far as they were concerned they held on their course, and they quietly and firmly informed the Bishop of Limerick that his political action had given grief and scandal to the Catholics (loud cheers). They had informed the Bishop that was an insult, not merely to the representatives of the Irish people, but to the most illustrious bishops and archbishops of Ireland, who were as cordially with them as any man in this country, and whose little finger was dearer to the heart of the Irish race than Dr. O'Dwyer's whole body (cheers). He could only hope that in every hour of danger for the Irish cause that Ireland would find as true men as the men of Limerick, and men who would act as bravely as they had done

MR. DILLON.

Mr. John Dillon, M.P.: He thought it would be plain to everyone in that room that those members of the Corporation of Limerick who voted against the resolution which was moved the other day, conferred a public benefit on the people of Ireland, because their action was the indirect cause of the holding of the meeting which had taken place that day, and in their blindness they threw down the challenge to the people of the South of Ireland which was taken up and answered in a fashion which he thought would satisfy those gentlemen (cheers). For his part, he rejoiced that that meeting had been held, and he thought they would believe
·01]

him when he said that as a cause for that rejoicing the smallest considerations were those as regarded his own conduct (hear, hear).   .   .   .   .

He came to accept the challenge which was levelled, not against his character, but against the policy which he had preached to the people of Ireland; and against the deadly attempt, so far as it lay with the man who made it, to shake and shatter the confidence which had been placed in the party of which he was a member by the people of Ireland, the confidence which had based and built up the present National power, which was the hope of, and the salvation of, the Irish people, and the destruction of which would involve the destruction of the people of this country (cheers). It was for that reason he came to Limerick, and that his friends came with him. They had accepted that challenge. It was never looked upon by him as a personal issue. The issue was this—Whether after ten years of splendid struggle, after success unparalleled in the history of Ireland, that now at the invitation of the Bishop of Limerick the people of this country should stop, should return to the basest form of Whiggery which they had emancipated them from, and crawl at the foot of any English Minister in power, and cast away the weapons which it was their pride and boast to have devised and placed in their hands, which for ten years they have used to such tremendous effect. That was the question and issue laid before the people of Munster that day, and they had answered with no hesitancy, and left no doubt, he trusted, on the public mind of this country (cheers).   .   .   .

Looking back over the history of the land question, was there in the whole history of mankind a more heartbreaking story? How many thousands, aye hundreds of thousands, of virtuous homes had been desolated, and their inhabitants reduced to slavery. Why? Because men like the Bishop of Limerick had shattered the organisation and the hopes of the people in the hour of their triumph. And when he saw the course that was being pursued by Bishop O'Dwyer, he said to himself, "Thanks be to God, the time had gone by when another brass band could be started in Ireland to ride triumphant to power and place on the smoking ruins of the homes of the tenantry in Ireland" (applause). In 1855 there were gallant men and able and self-sacrificing men fighting the cause of the Irish tenants, but in 1855, instead of one Castle bishop in Ireland, they had archbishops and bishops on the wrong side, which they had not now. **The people of Ireland would not give up boycotting and the Plan of Campaign at the dictation of an individual**; to-day there was not another bishop in Ireland, with perhaps one exception, who would

take his stand on that same policy, and who would dare to challenge
the policy of the Irish National Party (cheers). He thought they
had every reason to be thankful for that. At the time he thought
it was a good thing that this occasion should have arisen to show
to the whole world and to the people of England, and their own
in America and Australia, that there existed in the hearts of the
people of Ireland a spirit of independence which no outside power
can crush or put down, and in this great present movement for
Irish liberty those disasters and those misfortunes to which he had
alluded could not be, and never would be, repeated (cheers).—
Freeman's Journal, 25th August, 1890.

The *Freeman's Journal* is essentially the Parnellite
Catholic organ of Ireland; Catholic in one sense, but
exceedingly Parnellite (as will appear) in every other ;
it belongs to a company which is largely composed of
Irish Roman Catholic clergy. An analysis of the
shareholders show that out of 565 shareholders 100
are Catholic clergymen holding 2,229 of the ten
thousand £5 Preference Shares, Archbishops Walsh
and Croke being among the number. These few
words of explanation are necessary in order to intro-
duce the observations which are to be found in the
various leading articles of this paper upon the Limerick
scandal. On the 25th August, the day after the
Limerick demonstration, the *Freeman's Journal*, in a
long article upon this incident, contains the following
most characteristic sentence :—

And if he (the Bishop) have a plan, a practical plan, to effect
the national regeneration of Ireland before we are all in our
graves, in the name of common sense let him propound it and
work it out, and undergo labour and incur danger for it, and
prove by his works that he is as earnest and as good an Irishman
as John Dillon or William O'Brien. They are not wedded to
boycotting, if the Bishop have a surer and a swifter way which he
will work out with them, and which will have as practical results.
If he have not this plan, in the name, then, of truth, let the Bishop
of Limerick use all that he can of their plan, which they have
dared and suffered for, and use it with them and with his brethren
of the Episcopacy who are with them, and who are as good
Irishmen and as good Bishops as he is.
506]

It should be noted that, notwithstanding Dr. O'Dwyer's letter of the 26th July, already given neither in the speeches at Limerick, nor yet in the article just quoted, was there one single word spoken to deny, repudiate or explain the language against the Holy See which Mr. Dillon was so categorically accused to have used in the House of Commons on the 11th July, and against which the Bishop of Limerick had so eloquently protested. This important matter was completely and entirely ignored.

Dr. O'Dwyer, having read the proceedings which took place in Limerick on the 24th August, lost no time in writing the following letter, which appeared in the *Freeman's Journal* of the 26th August.

To the Editor of the "Freeman's Journal."

Limerick, 25*th August*, 1890.

Sir,—Notwithstanding the criticism of your article of to-day, I venture to think that a good body of Catholic opinion in Ireland will not endorse your judgment on yesterday's meeting, or regard it in any other light than as an attempt by popular intimidation to silence everyone who presumes to disobey the present leaders of politics in Ireland. Whatever be the merits of the controversy between Mr. Dillon and myself, I should like to know how far does the shouting of a multitude go to settle them. Whether I am a dastard or an unfaithful bishop to the people, or whether Mr. Dillon has acted ignobly in presence of the Coercion Act, I maintain it is an improper thing to come into a bishop's cathedral city and there by denunciations of him to rouse the passions of his people against him as a mercenary and a traitor, and if it is allowed to go without protest it will become a fatal precedent.

But what particularly I object to in yesterday's proceedings and in your article of to-day is the utterly unfair misrepresentation which precludes from the consideration of the public the great, solemn, and supreme issues that were raised by

MR. DILLON'S MEMORABLE SPEECH

in Parliament, by the clever plan of concentrating attention on the merest fringe of the whole controversy. Suppose that every charge that I am alleged to have made against Mr. Dillon and his colleagues was actually made by me and demonstrated to be false, and then that the whole of these parts of my letter was blotted out and judgment given against me upon them, does not enough remain to demand explanation from Catholic members of Parliament addressing a large Catholic assemblage, and from a Catholic newspaper such as the *Freeman* which might well be expected to attach due importance to them? But yet Mr. Dillon and Mr. O'Brien yesterday, and you, sir, to-day, make believe that the only question at issue is the personal honour of the Irish party; and getting a victory, as you think, on that, you shout that the whole cause is gained. The whole Catholic sense of this country was stirred by Mr. Dillon's unfortunate speech in the House of Commons. I do not suppose that you could find a Catholic in Ireland, lay or ecclesiastic, to defend it. So bad and indefensible was it that Mr. Dillon had the hardihood to deny that he ever spoke a whole sentence in which the poison was centred, and yet neither then nor even now, when you sit on the lofty eminence of your editoral chair in judgment upon us all, do you think it important enough for even the smallest reference. May I ask you, sir, again, if you have any recollection of publishing a short letter from me in which you printed side by side your own report and *Hansard's* of the sentence which Mr. Dillon denied having spoken, and, if so, whether in a fair appreciation of the controversy you might not have thought it necessary to note that

MR. DILLON HAS BEEN ABSOLUTELY SILENT

about the most damaging evidence against him? That was the one point in my indictment of him which he thought worthy of notice. All the rest he left loftily to the verdict of the Irish nation, and I suppose yesterday's meeting, and yet when he is convicted of a false statement in this denial he attempts to throw dust in the eyes of the public by personal issues, and you, sir, coolly observing the game, back him out in the manœuvre. But I take it that whatever explanation may be forthcoming consistent with Mr. Dillon's veracity, we may assume now, after yesterday's silence, that the line is drawn at Rome, and for the future the sacred person of the Vicar of Christ will be held above all attacks. That alone is something gained, although you may think very lowly of me as a bishop, I assure you in all honesty that I regard it as a result worth all the annoyance of achieving it. Towards the end of your article you invite me if I have a plan for the regeneration of my country to propound it. I discuss this, not for the purpose of scoring any point against you, but because it is a matter of very grave importance. I am not a politician. I have another profession. My mission is to teach to the people of the Christian religion the duties that it imports, and my interference, such as it has been, in public affairs, has been only in discharge of it. Now, soon after my consecration I was confronted with the practices of

BOYCOTTING AND THE PLAN OF CAMPAIGN,

and after the best consideration which I could give them I became convinced of their utterly sinful character. Soon a judgment followed exempt from the uncertainty with which I should necessarily regard my own. The Pope spoke. A decree sanctioned by him personally, and promulgated by the Holy Office by his command, was published absolutely condemning them. I have studied that condemnation to the best of my ability, and affirm on my responsibility that there is not in canon law or theology a shadow of a shade of grounds for doubting its binding force upon our consciences. Nay more, I am convinced it is my duty as a bishop, by every legitimate means in my power, to give effect to that teaching of the Head of the Church. I am within my rights in so doing. Not only that, but is it not my clear duty when the Pope has spoken on the question of moral law to enforce respect and obedience to his word? With me, then, it is not a question whether the Plan of Campaign and boycotting are effectual means for any end, but whether they are lawful means; and I tell you plainly that if the use of them freed Ireland from political thraldom to-morrow, and established a Parliament in Dublin, and diffused wealth and prosperity throughout the length and breadth of the land, I should say—I should have to say as a Catholic—we must not do evil that good may come. It is not a question that admits of compromise. It is one of right or wrong, and therefore it is altogether beside the issue to ask me to propound an alternative. You simply ask me to acquiesce in sin if I cannot find a more effectual way to success. That I will not do. If I were a simple priest in a parish I would stand aside and rigorously abstain from all interference in the politics of men who persist in

DEFYING THE HEAD OF THE CHURCH

and bringing his authority into contempt, but, being a bishop, I cannot without cowardice shirk the obligation of teaching my clergy and my people the course which they are bound to follow. Furthermore, to be very frank, I am distinctly of opinion that the persistence of the Irish people in disobedience to the Holy See, and worse, in the impugning of its authority, will, like a canker, eat into the heart of their faith, and leave it without vitality for the hour of trial that may come. Loyalty to Rome is the foundation of the Catholic system, and whoever impairs that is undermining the people's faith. The legend planted prominently on one of their banners read, "Our religion from Rome, our politics from home," and that sentiment has been the burden of Mr. Dillon's speech in the House of Commons, and of Mr. O'Brien's equally scandalous speech at Manchester. and is the underlying principle of yesterday's arguments. May I ask them what do

[509

they mean by religion? Are the Ten Commandments included in it? May Rome inform them authoritatively whether certain actions are violations of the Commandments as being against justice and charity? If not, then they mean, whatever they say, not only our politics, but our religion, from home. Private judgment for our actions, and we ourselves, and not the Pope, are to be the expounders of the moral law.

MR. O'BRIEN PROCLAIMS

"That Plan of Campaign which I have never hesitated to defend in the open day, and which I am prouder to-day than ever to defend from this platform." And that is his attitude in presence of a method which the supreme authority of the Church has condemned as unlawful, and when I refuse to associate myself with Catholics thus in revolt against the Head of the Church he charges me with "turning a question of politics into one of religion," and proclaims that he has shining in his political firmament ecclesiastics such as Dr. Croke and Dr. Walsh. Now, no man in Ireland has more reverence for those distinguished dignitaries than I have. But, even if it were true, as it is not, that Mr. O'Brien or Mr. Dillon had them on their side, I am not ashamed to say that I prefer to range myself with the Vicar of Christ.

It was in this connection that I interfered in the Glensharrold case. My principal concern for them was to get them out of a combination which they knew was condemned, and at the same time to obtain for them the most favourable terms. I had no motive but their good, and it is only the reckless malice of deliberate slanderers that can think of coupling my name with the landlord's interest in the matter. After long negotiations, the details of which I have already published, I obtained a settlement that I thought the people ought to accept. Practically, it wiped out over two thousand pounds arrears and permanently reduced the rent by over 50 per cent. but Mr. Dillon and his friends thought otherwise, and would not allow the tenants to settle unless they got five per cent. more. I said before, and I repeat it, that no sensible man will believe that such a course was taken simply in the interests of the poor tenants. The difference between what they were offered and what Mr. Dillon and Mr. O'Brien would accept amounted to £25 a year between forty-seven tenants, and I say that it was

CRUELTY OF THE VERY WORST TYPE

to these poor people to force them to undergo the sorrow of eviction for such a paltry sum. The people were anxious to settle. Just before I published my letter on the case I held my episcopal visitation in that parish. One of the tenants came to
510]

me by night with a list of the names of his fellow-tenants who were ready to pay their rents, to get my advice. I told him that, in my opinion, they would make a great mistake if they abandoned their holdings, and that they ought to pay. What do you think was the question he then asked, "If we pay will you protect us?" "Yes, I will," I said, "to the best of my ability," and it was for the purpose of exposing the unreasonable tyranny which was driving these poor people to destruction that I wrote the letter that Mr. Dillon has described in terms so becoming. And now that I have referred to the case, let me lay a few facts before the public that may interest those of them who understand agricultural affairs. "Is it not a hard case for me" said one of the tenants, "to have to leave my poor house." I inquired into his circumstances, and here they are taken down from his own lips. "I hold seventy-five acres of mountain land, on which I have fourteen milch cows, twelve two year olds, ten yearling heifers, three horses, and eight fat pigs, with plenty of turf." And what do you think is his rent under the terms I have got for him? Twenty pounds a year. I told him that he would be a lunatic to abandon such a holding and to go out upon the world. But what was it to Mr. Dillon and Mr. O'Brien, who are playing

A BIG GAME FOR POLITICAL STAKES,

if there was sorrow and heartbreak in that poor home? That tenant and several others have taken my advise, and are happy now, and wide is the difference between them and their poor evicted brethren.

There is first an explanation which I desire to add—first, with regard to the word "ostensibly" in my former letter. Although Mr. Dillon. after his indecent repetition yesterday of his insults spoken in the House of Commons, deserves little consideration at my hands. I think it right to say that I never meant to impute personal dishonesty to him, and then there is another phrase which I am told has given offence in quarters where I should be very sorry to offend. By the "crowd" with whom I would not associate, I meant those, and those only, who, as Mr. Dillon and Mr. O'Brien, advocate and defend the Plan of Campaign and boycotting in defiance of the condemnation of the Holy See. With such people I cannot enter into alliance. They may denounce me. They may hound on my people against me. I hold my authority not from politicians, not from the people, and while God spares me to govern this diocese I shall maintain, to the best of my poor ability, my own personal independence and the rights and prerogatives of the Vicar of Christ.

I am, sir, your obedient servant,
✠ EDWARD THOMAS,
Bishop of Limerick.

Thereupon the "Catholic" *Freeman's Journal* com. mented upon the letter as follows :—

[*Freeman's Journal* Article, 26th August, 1890.]

THE Bishop of Limerick falls back on the Pope this morning. It is his favourite manœuvre, and strategic, too, covering his retreat. But his Lordship is not content with getting behind the Papal throne. Picturing us "on the lofty eminence of the editorial chair," pronouncing judgment on everybody. Dr. O'Dwyer modestly perches himself on the top of the Castle of St. Angelo, and lays down the law *urbi et orbi* with a dogmatism which puts the Pontiff in the Vatican into a second seat. Is there, we ask, no orthodox Bishop in Ireland but his Lordship of Limerick? If Mr. Dillon and Mr. O'Brien and the other popular leaders who have incurred the Bishop's wrath be the rebels against spiritual authority described by Dr. O'Dwyer, how is it that nine-tenths of the twenty-eight Bishops are warm friends of those gentlemen? And wherefore, we wonder, is it that when opportunity presents itself the most distinguished in rank and fame of Dr. O'Dwyer's Episcopal brethren delight to do them honour? Are they all wrong? Is Dr. O'Dwyer alone right? Is everybody wrong but himself and Mr. Balfour? Far be it from us to chop theology, moral or otherwise, with the Bishop of Limerick. He is jealous of intrusion into his domain. He denies Mr. Dillon's right even to enter into his Cathedral City and venture to disagree with him. In the same breath he cries out that he is no politician. But what does he do? Being no politician, he turns a question of politics into a question of religion the moment the argument goes against himself. We are not so illiberal or so slippery as Dr. O'Dwyer. What Mr. O'Brien said on Sunday we repeat. Dr. O'Dwyer, the politician, has a perfect right to hold his own opinion about us, and the Irish people have just as good a right to hold their own opinion about Dr. O'Dwyer. But he is not content with that, for whenever he finds that the Irish people are not going to take their politics from him, he turns round and he clothes himself in the sacred garb of the Episcopacy, and he anathematises as an enemy to religion every man who differs from him, and he takes every attack that is made upon his own mischievous political pranks as if it were an attack upon the person of the Supreme Pontiff himself.

The Bishop is a doughty dialectician, and one never can be quite sure when he is in his political warpaint, and when clad in the Roman purple. Hey, presto! He changes with the magical celerity of a wizard. At one moment he is calling names like a fishwife. The next he hits you with the whole Ten Commandments. To-day he is in his Mount Sinai mood. For us, we go with the bulk of the Bishops. Of course we know that as soon as Dr. O'Dwyer puts on his feathers and takes tomahawk and scalping knife in hand, coming out on the political warpath, he will announce that he would not "go to Heaven" with that crowd. If he goes on as he is going he shall have to get a separate compartment even there. There is a story told of a man who was afflicted with a worrying wife, and who begged her one day to allow the Almighty to have something to do with the government of his own world. We pray Dr. O'Dwyer to imitate that good man by allowing the Almighty to have something to do with the government of His own Church.

And now to come down to the prosaic details of the Glensharrold Estate. The Bishop tells a tale, without names, with a sinister malignity which he knows will score across the Channel, and evoke such another article in the organ of the forger, perjurer, and suicide Pigott as that in which yesterday he is described by the *Times* as the one Prelate "who is standing unsupported in his own country as the champion of the Vatican." But if Mr. Dillon has wrought such miseries on Glensharrold homes is it not curious that when the honourable gentleman visited the place yesterday he was received with open arms, was greeted with a popular ovation, presented with an address, and that at a large public meeting the following resolution was adopted with every manifestation of the most cordial and genuine unanimity—

"That we, the tenants of the Glensharrold estate, having adopted the Plan of Campaign to resist the cruel and tyrannous treatment of our landlord, Mr. Delmege, hereby reiterate our determination to stand and adhere to our combination until victory crowns our cause."

The Irish members have no rewards and no honours to offer these poor people. Will the Bishop, who claims to be their benefactor, please explain how it is that he is received in frigid silence, and that John Dillon, who, according to his Lordship, has ruined them, is received with warm and unfeigned welcome? But we are glad to note by our report that John Dillon has not ruined them, and that, instead of the miserable hovels fit for pigs in which they are under notice of eviction, they have now provided for them substantial and comfortable stone cottages fit for men and women to live and thrive in. The truth is that, as Mr. O'Brien recounted on Sunday, the tenants on the Glensharrold estate had a cause so absolutely just that the Bishop himself was obliged through his Vicar-General to exempt them from the operation of Monsignor Persico's mission. According to Mr. O'Brien, in the only case in the diocese where the Plan of

Campaign was in force, the Bishop was obliged to admit that Monsignor Persico was absolutely wrong and that the Plan of Campaign was absolutely right. The Bishop saw he was in a dilemma, and he tried to get out of it by patching up an agreement of his own and forcing the tenants to adopt it. He went down unauthorised and uninvited, and he tried to intimidate the tenantry into accepting his agreement by telling them that their leaders would desert them and leave them to starve. He tried even to purchase their assent by offering to subscribe the sum of £100 to the sum they were to pay for their miserable rack-rents, and he did all that man could do openly and secretly to drag these tenants into an agreement which was condemned by his own valuer, Mr. Greene-Barry, and then what followed? He failed, as he invariably does. The people stuck to their leaders They stuck to their rights, and what happened ? Because these people, whose cause was so just that they were exempted from the strictures of the Rescript, these people who were so poor that he felt obliged to subscribe £100 to eke out their rack-rents, because these miserable, these wronged people refused to be led by him into an agreement condemned by his own valuer, the Bishop came out in the *Times* newspaper on the morning of the eviction campaign with a letter which was directly calculated to rob the Glensharrold tenantry of that English sympathy which he knew was their only safety and only protection against the blows of the exterminator. We now leave the Bishop to his own reflections. They cannot be very happy ones. His own people have struck against him as an incorrigible crank. He stands isolated amongst his Episcopal brethren. He has provoked the scandal of a vast public demonstration against him in his own Catholic and Cathedral City. He is covered with the compliments of the Coercion Press of England. He is the Irish Bishop of Beauvais, who handed over the deliverer of his people to the enemy, and consented to the burning of that deliverer at the stake in the name of religion. That deliverer is now honoured by Rome as well as by France. We respectfully called on his Lordship yesterday to prove his claim to patriotism by projecting a practical plan by which to win for Ireland the rights which are hers, or, if he could not, to fall into line with his brother Bishops and his people. His answer virtually is that he would not budge an inch from his present proud and straitlaced isolation if his moving would re-open the Irish Parliament in College-green to-morrow. Be it so. There is no more to be said. Let him be. We part from the Bishop with one kindly word. We are grateful and glad that his better nature has triumphed, and that he has the courage—no one denies him that quality, pity 'twere not for Ireland— to acknowledge that he has been unjust and wrong.

514]

I never meant," he writes, "to impute personal dishonesty to Mr. Dillon." We hope and trust that this ray of light may spread into a broad gleam of generous sunshine on the Bishop's heart and head, and that as his Lordship to-day regrets having been betrayed into hasty mis-judgments and expressions unworthy of him, so he shall be yet, if tardily, found on his people's side, this unpleasant episode of his life buried in oblivion.

Mr. Dillon went to Clonmel, a town outside the Limerick Diocese, and there, upon the 26th August, he delivered himself of the following speech, which is probably a still more remarkable and important one than that which he made at Limerick on the 24th. It will amply repay careful perusal.

MR. JOHN DILLON: I had hoped, and I had expected the meeting at Limerick the other day would have closed what to all Irish Catholics was a painful controversy. Painful it was, and humiliating, but, as I claim, humiliating not to us (cheers). We did not seek this controversy; it was forced upon us; and although I shall yield to no one in my respect for the ministers of my religion, and for the bishops of my church (cheers), I say here that, no matter what the consequence may be, that when a Catholic bishop comes out into the arena of politics and attacks with persistence, and in the most dangerous way, the great movement on which the homes and the very existence of our people are at stake, then if he were ten times a bishop I shall resist him (cheers). And while I shall make every effort to speak of the bishop with the respect due to his office, I shall treat his politics as if he were a Catholic layman; and I maintain, and I am prepared to prove, that in following that course I am treading in the steps of the most illustrious names that have ever shed honour on the Catholic laity of this country (applause). I am treading in the steps of O'Connell (applause), and I sincerely and deeply regret that by a publication of the most extraordinary character—as I think I shall prove—which appears in to-day's *Freeman's Journal*, the Bishop of Limerick has made it incumbent upon me to pursue this controversy somewhat further. In this morning's *Freeman's Journal* there appears a letter from his lordship, attacking not only myself but the *Freeman's Journal* also. What does his lordship do? He begins, or rather ends, his letter by stating that he thinks it right to say that "I never meant to impute personal dishonesty to Mr. Dillon." Then I do not know what the meaning of language is, nor does anyone else in Ireland, because if ever personal dishonesty of the basest kind

[515

was imputed to a man it was imputed to me (applause). But his lordship appears to be rather too late. After the meeting at Limerick takes place, he states that he does not impute motives of personal dishonesty to me, and never did. But what does he do then? He seeks in a letter extending to nearly two columns to shift his ground, and having absolved me from the charge of personal dishonesty, he now says that I am a liar (oh), and in the following way:—He says that the main subject of controversy between himself and myself has been ignored both by the *Freeman's Journal* and the speakers at the Limerick meeting. And what is the main subject of controversy now according to the bishop?—that I had assailed the Sovereign Pontiff in foul and offensive language, and he says the language was so bad and indefensible "that Mr. Dillon had the hardihood to deny that he ever spoke a whole sentence in which the poison was centred." Well, I did deny it, and the Bishop of Limerick having absolved me of personal dishonesty, now practically calls me a liar, because, he says, I did insult the Sovereign Pontiff. The morning after the speech was delivered I wrote to the papers to say that the whole of my speech was directed—as the context proves—to the action of the Tory Government in carrying on a base intrigue with Rome, and that I had not uttered one word in disrespect of the Sovereign Pontiff, and I went further and I said this—that if any language of mine uttered in the heat of debate in the House of Commons is open to such construction I now state that no such meaning ever entered into my mind, and that my language was entirely addressed to the action of Lord Salisbury and Mr. Balfour (applause).

REV. DEAN MAHONY, Sydney: I heard it, Mr. Dillon; you are perfectly correct.

MR. DILLON—I am very much obliged. An unexpected confirmation, for which I am most grateful, has come from one whom I will call a warm personal friend of my own—one of the most respected and venerated priests in Australia (applause)—who was sitting under the gallery in the House of Commons and listening to my speech. I ask you what other meaning could be attached to it? (Hear, hear.) The context of the speech proves what was in my mind. In order to avoid the possibility of a public scandal, I went so far as to say that if anything had escaped from my lips which could be twisted into the meaning of the charge Bishop O'Dwyer speaks of, I stated no such meaning entered into my mind, but that what I stated was directed at the intrigues of English agents in Rome; and I do, and I shall, denounce the intrigues which are going on at this hour, which are fraught with infinite danger to the Catholic religion of this country, and which I say it is the duty of priests and Catholic laymen alike in this country to guard against and watch (applause). Bishop O'Dwyer has plainly stated as the basis on which this letter was written that I falsely stated to the people of this country that I made no assault upon the Sovereign Pontiff. I leave it to the judgment of the Irish people whether I did not do all I could to remove the possibility of misconception arising on this most important point (hear, hear). I ask your special attention to this portion of his letter. I affirm, and I do so in cool blood, I am prepared to defend the proposition, that no more outrageous insult has ever been levelled against the whole Catholic episcopacy in Ireland and the priests, not to speak of the laity, than is contained in this letter of Dr. O'Dwyer. He says that "for the future the sacred person of the Vicar of Christ will be held above all attacks. That alone is something gained." Nobody said a word disrespectful of him as a bishop. I never did (applause). It is not my business to criticise him. The bishop goes on to state—"That alone is something gained; and although you may think very lowly of me as a bishop, I assure you in all honesty that I regard it as a result worth all the annoyance of achieving it." What does that mean? It means that I, speaking as the representative of a Catholic Irish constituency, assailed in the British House of Commons the Sovereign Pontiff, the Head of our Church, and that there was not found in Ireland one bishop, archbishop, or priest to defend the person of the Pope against my assault except Bishop O'Dwyer. In that letter is contained the charge that Dr. Croke (applause) the Archbishop of Dublin (applause), the Archbishops of Tuam and Armagh, stood silently by while I insulted the Pope, and never uttered a word in condemnation of the insult; that the Sovereign Pontiff had no champion in the whole of Ireland except Dr. O'Dwyer. I would feel a more bitter depth of humiliation than any Irish Catholic has ever been subjected to if the Sovereign Pontiff, the Head of our Church, had to look to Dr. O'Dwyer alone—a man of so little influence amongst his people—that he and the Delmeges were the only defenders and the only champions of the Pope. I say that in all the cruel history of insults and outrages levelled against the Church and the prelates of the Church, no more cruel insult was ever levelled against them than that the bishops stood silently by while the Head of the Church was assailed with opprobrium and insult. The bishop then goes on to illustrate what he objects to. He says that the legend planted prominently on a banner in the procession at Limerick was—"Our religion from Rome, our politics from home." I adopt these words (loud cheers): and I say they ought to be the words of every Catholic in this country, be he bishop, priest, or layman. I say it will be an evil day for the

Catholic religion in this country, and an evil day for the Irish race, when the bishops of Ireland find fault with such words as those (cheers). He also says that that principle was the basis of all the speeches made at Limerick, and "Mr. O'Brien's scandalous speech at Manchester." "May I ask these gentlemen," he writes, "what they mean by religion from Rome, and politics from home?" I answer the bishop by saying that what we mean is what O'Connell meant when he used precisely the same expression (cheers). Let me point out, too, that while O'Connell was fighting the great and hard battle which had been the charter of the liberty of the Irish Church—I mean the battle against the veto, which has preserved the Catholic Church in Ireland from many of the misfortunes which have overtaken it in Continental countries—he was denounced by Catholic bishops just as I am (cheers). There was a much stronger reason for denouncing O'Connell. And why? Because this policy of ours is not a question at all of Church discipline. We are merely asserting the right of the Irish representatives to carry on the political movement perfectly free from outside control (cheers). But O'Connell used these words, for which we are denounced because they appeared on a banner in a procession in which we took part, in reference to a question of Church discipline, in which he considered the liberties of the Irish Church were at stake, and therefore his words were much stronger. There is one other point in reference to this very valuable letter. He says no man in Ireland has more reverence for Dr. Croke and Dr. Walsh than he has. I don't think he has adopted a very wise way of showing it. He has endeavoured, so far as he could, to put them in a very cruel position. He has held them up before the people of Ireland as tacit assentors to insult levelled against the Holy See. In my humble judgment it would have been wiser for his own sake, and certainly he would have spared much pain in this Catholic country, had he left those who are his seniors in the Irish Church, who were bishops long before his name was heard of, and who are the leaders of the Irish Church, to defend the Holy See if the Holy See needed defence (hear, hear). I can only say that the day will never arise when the Holy See needs defence in Catholic Ireland (cheers). While we are determined to show to the world that we are independent in our politics, that we will not consent to have our political concerns made the subject of English intrigues either here in Ireland or any other part of the world, we, the Catholic laymen of Ireland, have proved in other ways and by greater sacrifice than is contained in the expenditure of printer's ink, that we are faithful to the Head of our Church (loud cheers). We have been faithful to the Church when it meant death and ruin in the past; we shall
518]

be faithful to the Church in the future; and I venture to say those of us who are strong Irish Catholics will be found, if ever a time of trial arises, as faithful as those that Dr. O'Dwyer calls "his crowd" (renewed cheers). Now, I have just a word or two to say. I don't like to detain this meeting too long (cries of "No, no," and "Go on.") But the matter is of such very great importance that I must say a few words on the history of the struggle on the Glensharrold estate, because a portion of his lordship's letter is devoted to that question, and would give to the public a most utterly false idea of the history of the struggle upon that estate. He says that we continued this struggle rather than accept a reduction of thirty-five per cent., and that the whole difference upon the estate between what we were going for and what the court was willing to offer was only £25. Now, what has been the history of the estate? Glensharrold is one of the poorest and most rack-rented estates in the West of Ireland; and from all I can gather there never was a body of tenants in this unfortunate part of the country subjected to greater robbery and persecution than were the tenantry on the Glensharrold estate. Now, no relief came to the Glensharrold tenants until we adopted the Plan of Campaign on the estate (applause). Up to that they had been harassed in every way that is known to the law for harassing Irish tenants, and when we had fought with the Plan of Campaign for two years on that estate, making sacrifices —some men going to jail—and considerable money being spent in maintaining the fight, the Bishop of Limerick, as he admits himself, for the purpose of getting the people out of their criminal combination, goes down to the estate and enters as negotiator between landlord and tenants behind our backs, and without consulting us at all. What was the result? Undoubtedly the landlord, anxious to secure the co-operation of Dr. O'Dwyer— the powerful co-operation of the bishop of the diocese—in bringing his tenants to a settlement, offered them terms which he never would have offered only for the Plan of Campaign (applause). The Bishop of Limerick sent down to the estate a valuer of the name of Mr. Barry, a gentleman who is looked upon all over Limerick as a landlord's valuer, and one whom the tenants would not think of employing. He goes over the estate as a friend of the bishop and the landlord's valuer, and he comes back with the report that the reduction which should be given was 40 per cent., the very reduction we had demanded from them (applause). Now what does the bishop do? He puts into his pocket and attempts to suppress the report of his own valuer which fully bore out our case, and recollect he is not the tenants' valuer, the probability being if we had a fair valuer he would have reported 60 or 70 per cent.—because it is perfectly valueless land, which I had an oppurtunity of seeing yesterday for myself—he puts it into his pockets and suppresses it; and from that hour to this we have never been able to get him to publish it. He then announces if the tenants will leave us and cease to be guided by our advice, and place their case in his hands, they will have a reduction of thirty-five per cent. and other concessions. That is to say, if the tenants give in and sacrifice the cause, sacrifice the men and policy by which they have obtained any concession and have been saved from ruin. and inflict to the best of their ability an injury to the cause of the tenants and us—and I say our prestige and power in Ireland is indissolubly bound up with the fortunes of the Irish tenants—he makes it a condition of their getting thirty per cent., that they break the combination, that they should publicly insult us by withdrawing from the Plan of Campaign, that he might triumph over us. Very well, that was the state of affairs when the case came before us. A gentleman came to our office in Dublin and stated he made this offer. Our reply was, "We will not counsel the tenants to drop their demand of 40 per cent. unless we have an assurance that if they do they shall get satisfaction." Remember the Bishop of Limerick's proposition was first that they should throw us over. and then that he would intercede to get them a reduction of 30 per cent. We said we would consent if a distinct assurance was conveyed to us that the 35 per cent. would be given to counsel the tenants to settle, therefore I don't think we were justified in doing more, as it was a great deal too little considering the circumstances of the estate, and that the priests were prevented from giving the people any assistance, and every effort was made to break up the combination and ruin the tenants. The reply we got was that the evictions were carried out. I ask you on whose head does the responsibility lie of carrying out these evictions for a difference of £25? Is it on our head (no) or on the head of the bishop and his allies? (Yes). They carried out these evictions without allowing the people to get the 35 per cent.. without making a surrender of the Plan of Campaign; therefore it is idle to talk about this difference of £25 being the only difference. So difficult were matters to be carried on. on account of the fact that the priests of the diocese were forbidden to speak to the unfortunate tenants, and partly from the fact that the tenants were so accustomed to oppression that they required a great deal of encouragement to urge them to keep up the battle. still with these and all other considerations in my mind I was anxious to settle the fight on the estate, but the terms offered did not in my judgment give a fair share of justice to the tenants. We could not consent to accept what was offered. We were justified in demanding, as we had spent a lot of money on the estate—we 520] were justified in compelling Mr. Delmege not only to place these tenants in a reasonable way to earn a living, but also to repay out of his rents some of the national funds we had been obliged to expend (applause). His lordship says, "Before I published my letter on the case I held my episcopal visitation in the parish. One of the tenants came to me by night with a list of the names of his fellow tenants who were ready to pay their rents, to go by my advice. I told him that in my opinion they would make a great mistake if they abandoned their holdings, and that they ought to pay. What do you think was the question he then asked? 'If we pay will you protect us?'" I think I have heard that before from police inspectors, and from land agents in the witness box in London, and it is perfectly true that on every poor estate in Ireland there are to be found men who either through cowardice or dishonesty are anxious to break away from the combination of their fellowmen. But recollect they are bribed to terms which never would have been offered to them but for that combination and the sacrifices of others, and I think it ill-becomes the Catholic Bishop of the diocese to lend himself to such proceedings (applause). I for one never sought for a moment to conceal or deny the fact that I am ready, and have always been ready, and have always warned the tenants to put such pressure as I often preach to the people of Ireland on any man who, having joined his fellowmen voluntarily in a combination for the assertion of their right and the salvation of their homes, seeks to make terms for himself outside that combination (hear, hear). Of course, there are dishonest sneaks on every estate in Ireland, and it is unfortunate that when things of this character do occur that they should be published to the world for the object of blackening our combination and robbing us of public sympathy by a Catholic bishop. That movement, I believe, in spite of all that is said in this letter, and of all the charges levelled against us from different quarters, is a movement based on justice, and on one of the highest principles which can combine together mankind—that is, on mutual loyalty (applause). It is a movement which, in my humble judgment, has done more to elevate the social condition and politically to emancipate the people of Ireland in ten years than all the gallant sacrifices of the previous hundred years (applause). It is a movement which, in my judgment, also has taught the people of Ireland more of mutual confidence and more of self-reliance than any movement that has gone before it, and in spite of these denunciations and in spite of these charges, so long as I retain the confidence of an Irish constituency, so long shall I continue to preach these principles to the people of Ireland, until the accursed load of landlordism and foreign-made laws is rolled from off the necks of our people. And this I will only say in conclusion, that I repeat once more the challenge which his lordship in his letter to-day refuses to meet. If he has fault to find with our methods and our policy let him propose better methods (applause). **I should be ashamed to take part with a people who, having seen the goal and the aim of their agitation almost realised, should suddenly be conscience-striken in using boycotting against Irish landlordism** (applause). When did his lordship, or any man of his stamp, ever find an occasion to denounce the exterminators of the people of Ireland? (Applause). They were silent when Delmege was robbing the Glensharrold tenants, but their consciences prick them when the Glensharrold tenantry try to boycott Delmege (hear). Well. I believe the conscience of the Irish people is pure in this matter (applause). I believe the Irish people will continue this policy as long as the necessity arises (applause). It is a blessing to the people of Ireland, and it will be their salvation (renewed applause), and in spite of the condemnation of Bishop O'Dwyer I believe they will continue to use that weapon until they bring to pass the complete emancipation of their race (prolonged applause).

The reader will have doubtless noted that Messrs. O'Brien and Dillon, followed by the *Freeman's Journal,* laid great stress upon the allegation that the Bishop of Limerick in his dealings with the Glensharrold tenantry had repudiated the opinion of his own valuer [a gentleman named Mr. Greene-Barry]. This attack, however, signally failed, as the following telegram, sent by Mr. Greene-Barry to the *Freeman's Journal* and published by that paper on the 27th August, will show. Incidentally, too, this telegram will also afford the reader a measure by which he can estimate the value of Parnellite utterances of a like nature. Mr. Greene-Barry telegraphed :—

To the Editor of the "Freeman."

Statement in your leader this day that I condemned the settlement proposed by Dr. O'Dwyer in Glensharrold dispute is not the fact. On the contrary, I thought the Bishop's proposal just and equitable, and think so still. James Greene-Barry.

43

The *Freeman* of the 27th August has some remarks
upon Mr. Dillon's speech at Clonmel and upon the
situation which deserve attention.

In matter and in manner Mr. Dillon's speech is a model of
cogent, calm, modest, and rational reply to the Bishop of
Limerick. . . . Of Bishop O'Dwyer we can only speak in
sorrow—certainly not in anger. The great and holy Prelates to
whom Mr. Dillon alludes hold their commissions from exactly
the same exalted source as that upon which he dilated with so
much aggressiveness in his letter. They are Mr. Dillon's friends.
They are our friends, we are proud to say, and never shall that
trust and friendship, we trust, be forfeited. They are above all
the people's friends and the foes of the people's foes. The Bishop
of Limerick might well reflect upon the company in which he is
found in this controversy.

The scandal was now complete. A Bishop had
taken upon himself the painful but conscientious duty
of teaching his people morality. He had been
denounced by the professional patriots in no measured
language for his legitimate action. He had suggested
to these " patriots " that if they thought him wrong in
his theology, they could satisfy themselves upon this
point by an appeal to Cardinal Manning in London,
or to any Catholic Bishop in Ireland. The answer he
got to this request was characteristic to men who are
in the wrong, and who know they are in the wrong.
They heaped insult upon him, they assailed his sacred
office, and they attempted to defeat his efforts to do
what he believed to be his duty to his Diocese.
Furthermore, both " patriots " and " patriotic " press
loudly declared that Dr. O'Dwyer was alone, and that
the rest or great bulk of the Irish Bishops approved of
their action. The moment was, doubtless, a critical
one, and hitherto no colleague of the Bishop of
Limerick had opened his lips ; on the 27th August,
however, the Archbishop of Dublin broke the silence.
He wrote a letter to the *Freeman's Journal* which was
published on the 28th. This letter has given rise to

considerable criticism, and should be read with care. It is as follows:—

To the Editor of the "Freeman."

"Dear Sir,—I feel that the good sense of the Catholics of Ireland, whether laymen or ecclesiastics, will bear me out in my view that I am called upon to make a very earnest protest against the use that has been made of my name in the course of the angry dispute now ranging in the south of Ireland.

"The matter of which I have to complain being of the most public occurrence, I feel that my protest also should be publicly made.

"I shall probably be absent from Ireland for the next few weeks. In my absence I shall not have a fair chance of speaking out for myself, as I should undoubtedly feel called upon to do, if this novel species of public controversy, involving the use of my name as a weapon whether of attack or defence, were to go on much longer. I trust, then, that if this unhappy wrangle is to be continued, those directly concerned in it will see the propriety of paying what respect they can to my now publicly expressed protest against the dragging of my name into a dispute with which, in any of its aspects—political, personal, or otherwise controversial—I have nothing whatever to do.

"I remain, dear sir, most faithfully yours,
"William J. Walsh,
"Archbishop of Dublin."

The Archbishop was reported in the same paper to have left Ireland on the 27th, his destination was not announced.

This pamphlet is concluded by recording one other event, which happened eight days after the Limerick scandal, and which is published in the *Freeman's Journal* of the 2nd September. It is given without comment.

This afternoon (Monday, 1st September) Mr. John Dillon M.P., and Mr. William O'Brien, M.P., arrived at Thurles to visit the Archbishop of Cashel, who invited them to spend a few days with them prior to their departure for America. The visit was intended to be of a private character, but the irrepressible people of Tipperary no sooner heard of it than they had a magnificent demonstration to greet them. The party left Dublin by the one
524]

o'clock train, and at various stations along the route where they were recognised they were cheered. Upon the arrival of the train at Thurles an enormous crowd had assembled on the platform. Amongst those present were Rev. N. Rafferty, Adm., and some eight other priests. A telegram was received from Mr. Thomas Condon, M.P., stating that he was unable to attend.

THE REV. MR. RAFFERTY, Adm., who was moved to the chair, said he felt he could dispense on this occasion with the usual formality of introducing the gentlemen they had come to welcome and honour (cheers). There were no two living Irishmen of our time better known and more loved and more trusted by the whole Irish race for unflinching and chivalrous advocacy of the cause of Irish nationality than John Dillon and William O'Brien, and no two living Irishmen more feared by their opponents (cheers). The present visit of Mr. Dillon and Mr. O'Brien to the Archbishop was one of a purely friendly and private character, but he was thankful to see the spontaneous and extraordinary demonstration of welcome that awaited them at the hands of the assembled thousands he saw around him (cheers), who evidently were unwilling or unable to repress their feelings of affection and enthusiasm for the most cherished and devoted advocates of the Irish cause (cheers).

MR. WILLIAM O'BRIEN, M.P., who was received with loud cheers, said—Fellow countrymen, you are aware that we are here as the guests of your illustrious Archbishop, Dr. Croke (cheers).

MR. JOHN DILLON. M.P., who was received with cheers, said—Men of Tipperary, I am proud to be here once more in the old Town of Thurles, where I often stood during the course of the last ten years. I am prouder still to be here as the guest of his Grace the Archbishop of Cashel (cheers).

Mr. O'Brien and Mr. Dillon then proceeded to the Archbishop's palace, where they were received by his Grace.

www.ingramcontent.com/pod-product-compliance
Lightning Source LLC
Chambersburg PA
CBHW021430090426
42739CB00009B/1435